SURPRISE, TROJANS!

THE STORY OF THE TROJAN HORSE

by Joan Holub
illustrated by Dani Jones

Ready-to-Read

Simon Spotlight

New York   London   Toronto   Sydney   New Delhi

Dear kids,

Long ago, Greeks wrote stories called myths. These stories helped them to understand things that were happening in the world around them. Myths also taught lessons about right and wrong. Some characters in mythology do things that are impossibly amazing or flat-out wrong to help teach us what *not* to do in real life!

—J. H.

SIMON SPOTLIGHT
An imprint of Simon & Schuster Children's Publishing Division
1230 Avenue of the Americas, New York, New York 10020
Text copyright © 2014 Joan Holub
Illustrations copyright © 2014 Dani Jones
First Simon Spotlight edition November 2014
For information about special discounts for bulk purchases, please contact Simon & Schuster Special Sales at 1-866-506-1949 or business@simonandschuster.com.
The Simon & Schuster Speakers Bureau can bring authors to your live event. For more information or to book an event contact the Simon & Schuster Speakers Bureau at 1-866-248-3049 or visit our website at www.simonspeakers.com.
Manufactured in the United States of America 1014 LAK
2 4 6 8 10 9 7 5 3 1
Library of Congress Cataloging-in-Publication Data
Holub, Joan, author.
Surprise, Trojans! : the story of the Trojan horse / by Joan Holub ; illustrated by Dani Jones. — First Edition.
pages cm. — (Ready-to-read)
1. Trojan horse (Greek mythology)—Juvenile literature. 2. Trojan War—Juvenile literature.
I. Jones, Dani, 1983- illustrator. II. Title.
BL820.T75H65 2014
398.20938'02—dc23
2013047985
ISBN 978-1-4814-2087-7 (hc)
ISBN 978-1-4814-2086-0 (pbk)
ISBN 978-1-4814-2088-4 (eBook)

Thousands of years ago, the Greeks played a big trick on the Trojans during a war. Greek writers said it happened like this.

King Menelaus ruled
the city of Sparta in Greece.
His queen was named Helen.

Menelaus: men-uh-LAY-us

King Priam ruled
the city of Troy in Turkey.
He had a son named Paris.

Priam: PRI-um

One day, Paris fell in love
with Helen and took her to Troy.

This made King Menelaus mad!
He asked two Greek kings named
Odysseus and Agamemnon
to help get her back.

Odysseus: oh-DISS-ee-us
Agamemnon: ag-uh-MEM-non

The three kings and their Greek army sailed to Troy.

When they landed,
soldiers called Trojans ran out
of the city to meet them.
A battle began.
Swords clashed. Arrows flew.
It was war!

The Trojan War went on for ten
years.
Many soldiers fought and died
on both sides.
Odysseus wanted to win.
It would not be easy.

There was a tall, strong stone wall
around Troy to protect it.
Trojan guards stood atop the wall
to watch for enemies.
If only the Greeks could
get through the wall!

The Greeks were good
at building wooden ships.
That gave Odysseus an idea.
His soldiers cut down trees
and sawed them into boards.
They built a big wood frame.

Then they covered the frame
with a skin of wood boards.
What were they building?
The Trojans did not know.

The Greeks had built a horse statue!
It was giant size.
Maybe even taller than
the wall around Troy.
The horse was hollow inside
and had a door
on its belly.

Odysseus and some soldiers
climbed through the door.
They hid inside the horse's belly.

The rest of the Greeks sailed away.
All except one.
His name was Sinon.
He hid near the horse and waited.

When the Trojans saw
the Greek ships go,
they were happy.
They had won the war!
Or so they thought.

They ran down to the battlefield.
They spotted the horse.
Some Trojans wanted to burn it.
Others voted to chop it up
or drown it in the sea.

Then Sinon spoke up.
He told them the horse was a gift
for the goddess Athena.
He said the Greeks had built it
so she would keep them safe
on their trip home.
This was not true.

The Greeks had built the horse
to fool the Trojans!
The Trojans fell for the trick.
They decided it would be
bad luck to ruin this special gift.

King Priam's daughter, Cassandra,
said the horse would bring trouble.
But no one listened.
The Trojans rolled logs under
the big horse and added wheels.

They pushed and pulled.
They brought the horse
through the gate
and into the city of Troy.

That night, the Trojans had a party.
They sang and danced.
They ate and drank.
Soon, they fell asleep.
The night got quiet and dark.

Creak!

The door in the horse's belly opened.

Odysseus and his Greek soldiers slid down a rope.

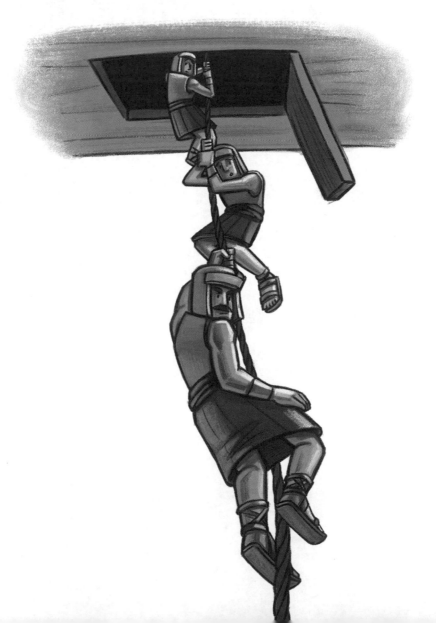

They landed on the street.
They had made it inside
the walls of Troy at last!

The Greeks climbed up the wall
and lit torches.
It was a secret sign.
The rest of the Greek soldiers
were waiting on a nearby island.

They had not gone home after all.
Now they rushed back to Troy.
They ran in through the gates.
It was a surprise attack!

Some Trojans got away.
But many others were killed.
The whole city of Troy burned
down.
The Greeks had won the war!

They found Helen and sailed for
home.
It would take Odysseus
ten more years
to get back to Greece.

Because of the Trojan horse,
there is a famous saying today.
It goes like this:
Beware of Greeks bearing gifts!